RoSPA
DRIVER
SERVICES

The Official Guide to the LGV Test

PA LGV TEST

C000003839

GORDON COLE

IAN ALLAN
Publishing

First published 1993

ISBN 0 7110 2174 0

© Gordon Cole 1993

Designed by Ian Allan Studio

Published by Ian Allan Publishing,

an imprint of Ian Allan Ltd, Terminal House, Station Approach, Shepperton, Surrey TW17 8AS; and printed by Ian Allan Printing Ltd, Coombelands House, Coombelands Lane, Addlestone, Weybridge KT15 1HY.

Introduction

This is the latest volume in a series of driving manuals by the author. They all convey their information through sequences of pictures of actual driving situations, with explanatory captions and text couched in simple direct language, instead of the customary mass of text and few illustrations. The contents of these pages explain and show the syllabus for the Large Goods Vehicle (LGV) Test. This test has been designed to comply with the specific criteria that correspond with the objectives of the Commission of the European Community.

To pass the LGV test, the trainee driver has to prove to an examiner that he/she can demonstrate, throughout the test, the ability to comply with the required criteria. The driver must be able to drive a vehicle safely in different types of traffic and on various types of roads. The driving test is part of the process that takes potential drivers from the training stage through to being qualified to drive LGVs unsupervised on the public highways. The most positive way that this can be achieved is through professional instruction — for which there is no substitute. A book of this nature can assist the candidate to appreciate more fully the skills required and the techniques adopted, but nothing can really prepare the candidate for the test better than practical experience and proper tuition.

The information in this book is not only designed to help the trainee to pass the LGV test, but also to give a better appreciation of the particular skills required to handle an LGV — hopefully, thereby, to prevent future accidents. This can be achieved by ensuring that drivers adopt the same rules, and apply them whenever the situation demands. There are more skills required for driving an LGV than for a car — as you will learn as you progress through these pages.

Other books by Gordon Cole:

Apart from *Pass the LGV Test*, Gordon Cole has written a number of other driving books that will be of interest to readers of this book.
- **Pass the Driving Test**: a detailed exploration of the techniques required to pass the standard Department of Transport driving test.
- **Advanced Driving**: the official RoSPA guide to advanced driving, which explains in depth the 'system' of motoring.
- **Safer Motorway Driving**: a guide to the particular skills required when driving on Britain's congested motorway network.

All three are published by Ian Allan Publishing and are available from all good bookshops. In the event of any difficulty, copies can be obtained from Bookpoint Ltd (telephone: 0235 831700) quoting reference numbers 9169, 1317 and 9649 respectively.

Contents

Types of LGV

Right:
A 17-tonne rigid unit.

Below right:
Drawbar trailer: 12 tonnes gross.

Bottom:
12-tonne articulated unit; 28 tonnes gross.

Acknowledgements

I would like to thank the following Police forces for their co-operation; without it, some of the photographs would have proved impossible to take:

Hertfordshire Constabulary
Bedfordshire Police
Metropolitan Police

A special thank you is also due to the Directors and staff of Metro School of Motoring for the use of the company's vehicle and time during the preparation of the book. The company can be contacted at:

204 Hampton Road West,
Hanworth,
Middlesex TW13 6BG.
Telephone: 081-893 4515.

I am also very grateful to Derek Lydiatt of the Wallace School of Motoring.

The line drawings on pages 14, 15 and 41 are reproduced from *Advanced Vehicle Technology* by Heinz Heisler published by Hodder & Stoughton by kind permission of the publishers.

All photographs were taken by the author using Leica cameras and lenses. Developing and printing was undertaken by The White House (081-866 0006).

For further information on fleet training in association with RoSPA, please contact the author on 0438 815203.

Figure 1:
Elementary driver function model.

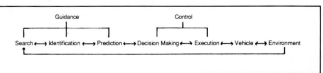

1 The Requirements of an LGV driver

Driving a Large Goods Vehicle today needs a good deal of knowledge and skill. Safety has to be the first consideration, and you must exercise the highest degree of courtesy, tolerance and consideration for all other road users, including pedestrians, and never forget the weight, size and length of a vehicle nor the weight and distribution of its load.

By law you must be 21 or over to drive a Large Goods Vehicle, unless you hold an LGV trainee driver's entitlement. The age of 21 is considered to be that of maturity; young male drivers in particular commit a higher proportion of traffic offences than any other demographic group, although in fairness some young male drivers are extremely competent. Motoring behaviour is likely to be learned at an early age; for example an irresponsible driving style of a parent or enthusiasm for motor sport is often imitated, and there is often a belief that the ability to handle a vehicle at speed creates higher social esteem — it's good for your 'street cred'! This combined with lack of training, experience and knowledge of the vehicle being driven, are all contributory factors to a high accident rate amongst young drivers. Hence the minimum age limit of 21 to drive an LGV.

Most road accidents are caused by human error. This can take various forms; not looking and thinking ahead, not recognising conditions which could lead to an accident, taking the wrong course of action, lack of concentration or tiredness. Trainee LGV drivers need to approach the task of learning driving skills with a responsible attitude; a sloppy, 'couldn't care less' attitude to the textbook way of driving a vehicle or contempt for the advice given in the Highway Code is a recipe for failure. Some trainees have a natural ability to learn; others may never be able to acquire the skills necessary to pass the LGV driving test.

Apart from learning to make proper use of the controls of the vehicle, smoothly, at the right time and place, the successful LGV driver must learn to read the road, take appropriate action and make the right decisions.

Reading the road

This can be broken down into three elements: search, identification and prediction. These inform the driver where and when to look, and what to look for, enabling an accurate assessment to be made. They answer the questions:

Is there any potential danger that could influence my driving?

What is it?

What can be expected to happen?

Search is simply looking out for any hazard or circumstance which is likely to require a response.

Identification is the classification of these observations according to their information content.

Prediction involves the anticipation of changes of conditions and circumstances in the immediate vicinity, and the movement and volume of traffic from available information.

Efficient and accurate judgement of these give the driver the ability to assess the current driving situation quickly, and to predict the potential dangers, thereby maximising the time available to act on the information given and assisting him/her to continue his/her journey safely and efficiently.

The driver needs to be able to recognise and understand a given situation, and to be able to implement a correct course of action. He/she should be able to proceed at a rate and direction partly self-paced and partly determined by circumstances, and to maintain a safe distance from other vehicles and objects.

The driver has to match changes of circumstances by using the appropriate controls to maintain/select the correct speed, direction of travel and separation distance from the vehicle ahead. The road ahead might change direction and start to climb, requiring the driver to turn the steering wheel and change the amount of pressure on the accelerator. The driver must compensate for the road topography, surface, traffic signs and signals, junctions, other vehicles and pedestrians, physical objects, and the vehicle being driven. (see figure 1)

2 Provisional licence entitlement and medical examination

Before you can drive an LGV on the public highway, you need a provisional driving licence. You will have to apply for this entitlement for the category of vehicle you intend to drive. Large Goods Vehicles come under the categories of C (rigid) and E (articulated/drawbar) — see figure 2. To be able to apply for an LGV provisional licence, you must have passed and be in possession of a full driving licence for a category B (car/light van) vehicle. As from 1 April 1994 higher weight (mass) of test vehicles will apply. Therefore a vehicle used for an LGV driving test for category C will need to be at least 11 tonnes and for category E at least 21 tonnes. This is also shown in figure 2.

At one time, for example, a trainee driver could be what was termed a double 'L' driver. This meant that one provisional licence was required and that, on passing the driving test on any category HGV, they automatically acquired the old group 'A' (now category 'B') driving licence. That practice has now been stopped and, as a result, a test for each category of vehicle must now be passed. There is one exception where, on passing the LGV driving test on a category 'E' vehicle, the candidate will also acquire a category 'C' entitlement.

To obtain an application form for an LGV (or Passenger Carrying Vehicle) provisional licence you will have to apply for a form entitled *Application for Large Goods Vehicle (LGV) or Passenger Carrying (PCV) Entitlement* (form D2). You will also need another form entitled *Medical Examination* (form DTp 20003). A medical examination has to be completed by a doctor on an applicant for Large Goods Vehicle or PCV driving licence. These forms can be obtained from: The Driver Enquiry Unit, DVLA, Swansea, SA6 7JL (telephone: 0792-772151). A call queuing system is in operation. If a ringing tone is obtained, wait for an answer as calls are taken in turn.

When you receive the Medical Examination form (DTp 20003) you must comply with the instructions stated as to which sections of the form the candidate has to complete. You will have to undergo a medical examination to make sure you are fit to drive an LGV. The doctor will, therefore, complete those sections of the form that relate to the actual medical examination. Your weight,

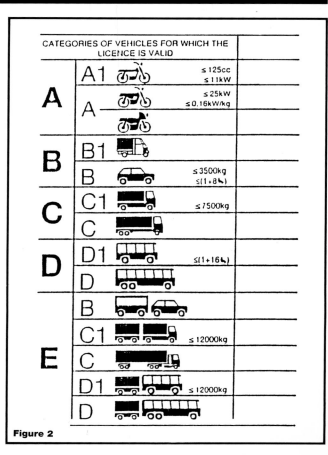

CATEGORIES OF VEHICLES FOR WHICH THE LICENCE IS VALID		
A	A1	≤ 125cc ≤ 11kW
	A	≤ 25kW ≤ 0.16kW/kg
B	B1	
	B	≤ 3500kg ≤ (1 + 8↖)
C	C1	≤ 7500kg
	C	
D	D1	≤ (1 + 16↖)
	D	
E	B	
	C1	≤ 12000kg
	C	
	D1	≤ 12000kg
	D	

Figure 2

height and eyesight will be checked. The eyesight test is and must be thorough. By law a licence may not be issued if the applicant has a visual accuracy worse than 6/9 in the better eye or worse than 6/12 in the other eye or, if corrective lenses are worn, has an uncorrected acuity in either eye of less than 3/60.

The Medical Examination form explains in detail the medical aspects of a candidate's fitness to drive an LGV. When your medical examination has been satisfactorily completed, you should send the medical form together with the application for the LGV provisional licence (form D2), your full motor car driving licence or, in the case of your provisional licence, your test pass certificate, and the appropriate fee. As driving licence fees are subject to periodic review, you should ask your instructor or contact The Driver Enquiry Unit at DVLA Swansea (telephone: 0792-772151) to find out the present day cost for the appropriate licence you need and any other up-to-date information you may need to know. Send your application for an LGV licence to:

First Provisional LGV,
The Vocational Team,
DVLA,
Swansea SA99 1BR.

If this is your first application for category C or E entitlement, you must wait for your licence to arrive before you begin to drive these types of vehicles on the public highway. When you get your licence you can start your driver training. Your instructor will explain all the controls and other components relating to driving an LGV. The trainee driver must always be aware that the skills required in handling LGVs, even such mundane aspects as entering and leaving the vehicle, differ significantly from those of the ordinary motor car. We will examine these skills in detail in later chapters.

3 Applying for an LGV driving test

Before applying for a test, make sure your general ability to drive an LGV is up to the required standard. You must demonstrate a high standard of competence in handling the vehicle, and have appreciation of the mechanical principles involved in driving it safely. You must also have a detailed knowledge of, and be able to apply, the rules of the *Highway Code* and be able to identify a selection of traffic signs and road markings. You must show that, generally, you have a full understanding of the principles involved in driving Large Goods Vehicles and of the application of these principles. You must also be able to demonstrate proper control in a wide variety of situations. Because of the size and weight of Large Goods Vehicles, their drivers must have a highly developed level of consideration for other road users; otherwise you cannot be considered a fit person to hold a vocational driver's licence. If you can comply with these requirements, you should apply for an LGV driving test.

To apply for a test you will need to complete an application for a Large Goods Vehicle (LGV) Driving Test Appointment (Form DLV 26), which can be obtained from any Driving Standards Agency (DSA) Regional Office. A list of these offices can be seen at the back of this book. Study the notes for guidance on the form carefully. Always provide all the particulars requested, otherwise the form will have to be sent back to you. This could lead to your appointment for a test being delayed. Send your application at least 28 days before the day you wish to be tested, with a cheque or postal order (keep the counterfoil) made payable to 'Driving Standards Agency' and send it to the DSA office in the region which covers the test centre for which you are applying.

4 How to get in and out of a Large Goods Vehicle

How to get out of the vehicle

Above:
Before considering opening the door, the mirrors must be used. The driver will, thus, be aware of any traffic approaching from the rear. If traffic is seen in the mirrors, you have no option but to wait until it has passed. Should a continuous flow of traffic be seen, it will be safer and quicker to leave the vehicle from the nearside. If alighting from the nearside, it is equally important that the driver checks to make sure that there are no pedestrians, or other potential hazards, in the vicinity.

Right:
If no traffic is seen in the mirrors, check any blind spots and then look to the front to make sure it is safe to open the door. If it is safe to do so, open the door, bearing in mind the situation can change before completing your exit.

One aspect of driving, which is taken for granted by numerous drivers every day, is the way in which the vehicle is entered and left. Some drivers open the cab door without checking that it is safe to do so; this can lead to a potentially dangerous situation resulting in the possibility of serious injury to the driver or others, apart from possible damage to vehicles. Some drivers have been seen jumping out of their vehicle and, in consequence, have injured themselves and others. Indeed, there are instances where the jump has proved fatal. Lack of concentration, complacency, negligence or stupidity have been the cause of numerous accidents. The following pictures show and explain the correct procedures that should be adopted, not only for the test but throughout your driving career. When the vehicle has been brought to rest, properly secured and the engine stopped, the driver should use the mirrors in order to check the position of traffic approaching from behind. If it is safe to open the door and alight from the cab, then do so using the foot-rests and guide rails provided. If the traffic situation so warrants, the driver should wait until the situation has changed.

It is equally important that the driver takes all round observation before re-entering the cab. When doing so, it is also imperative that the handrails are used properly whilst climbing into the cab. The temptation to use the steering wheel as an additional aid to entry should be resisted.

Far left:
Open the door. When the door is open take another look, as before, to make sure it is still safe to leave the cab.

Bottom left:
If it is safe, position your body and hold the guide handrails as shown.

Left:
Use each step provided to descend from the cab. Slide your hands down the handrail, after you have reached a lower step.

Right:
**It is important to keep
looking whilst descending
from the cab.**

Far right:
**When you have reached
ground level, close the door.
Then walk to the front of the
vehicle. By going to the front
of the vehicle the driver
reduces the risk of injury
caused from any passing
traffic.**

How to get in the vehicle

Far left:
If the vehicle has been unattended for some time, the driver should, before entering the cab, walk the length of the vehicle to check that it has not been tampered with; also check that all dropsides and the tailboard (if fitted) are properly fastened. Make sure children are not playing under the vehicle. Always make sure that all is safe before attempting to move off. The driver in this photograph has checked the vehicle and is making sure it is safe to climb into the cab.

Left:
Before opening the door make sure it is safe to do so, by looking to the rear then front for approaching traffic.

Right:
Whilst opening the door, the driver continues to check that it is safe to climb into the cab.

Far right:
The driver should continue to be alert for any potential danger while ascending the foot-rests into the cab.

Far left:
The driver is concentrating on entering the cab. Note how the handrails, and not the steering wheel, are being used to assist the driver.

Left:
Once in the cab, the driver will turn his body on to the seat and make sure it is safe to close the door.

5 Uncoupling and recoupling an articulated vehicle

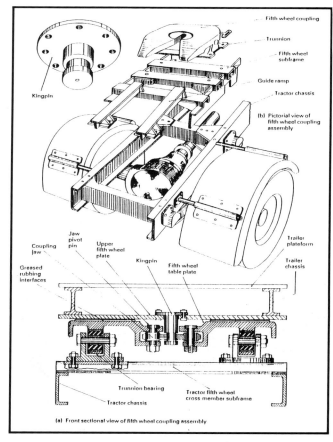

Trainee drivers of articulated vehicles must know how to uncouple and recouple a tractor unit from a semi-trailer. A driving test candidate will be asked by the examiner to explain the procedure for uncoupling and recoupling a semi-trailer at the start of the test. This question is part of the test and must therefore be answered in detail. The candidate should be able to point out and explain the various components but will not actually have to uncouple the unit as part of the test. The reason the candidate is asked this question, at the start, and other questions relating to the vehicle at the end of the test, is to test his/her knowledge on the subject. Some candidates arrive at the test centre with little or no idea of their responsibilities when in charge of a Large Goods Vehicle. Without this knowledge there is the potential of danger to both the LGV driver and to other road users.

When a candidate is being tested on an articulated vehicle or one drawing a trailer, his/her knowledge of uncoupling and recoupling the semi- or drawn trailer safely will be tested orally. About six questions will be asked, as appropriate, on the correct sequence of operation and the safety factors involved.

Fifth wheel coupling assembly

The fifth wheel coupling attaches the semi-trailer to the tractor unit. It consists of a semi-circular table plate with a central hole and a 'vee' section cut-out towards the rear. Underneath this plate are a pair of pivoting coupling jaws. The semi-trailer has an upper fifth wheel plate under the chassis, with a downward-facing kingpin. When the trailer is coupled to the tractor unit, this upper plate rests and is supported on the top of the tractor fifth wheel table plate with the two halves of the coupling jaws engaging with the kingpin. To allow the coupling to swivel, the faces of the tractor fifth wheel table and trailer upper plate should be heavily greased. Thus, although the trailer articulates about the kingpin, its load is carried by the tractor table.

Figure 3: right:
Fifth wheel coupling assembly.

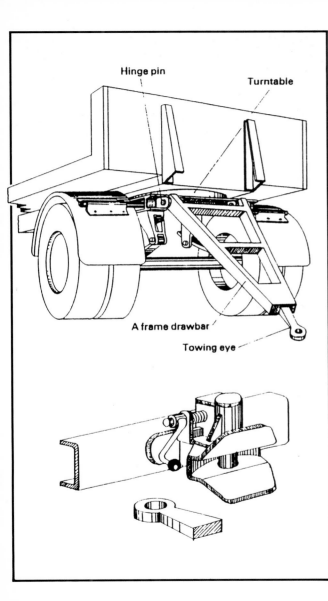

Hinge pin

Turntable

A frame drawbar

Towing eye

Trailer drawbar couplings

Drawbar trailers are normally hitched to the tractor unit by an 'A'-frame drawbar, which is coupled by means of a towing eye formed on the end of the drawbar. When coupled, the towing eye hole is aligned with corresponding holes in the upper and lower jaws of the tractor unit coupling, and an eyebolt passes through both coupling jaws and drawbar eye to complete the attachment. Lateral drawbar swing is permitted owing to the eye bolt pivoting action and the slots between the jaws on either side. Aligning the towing eye to the jaws is made easier by the converging upper and lower lips of the jaws, which guide the towing eye as the tractor unit is reversed.

The following pictures and text show and explain the procedure for uncoupling and recoupling a semi-trailer.

Uncoupling

Before starting to uncouple, the driver must make sure the trailer is in a safe place which complies with the law and the chosen area must be flat and firm. If these requirements are met, the vehicle can be stopped and the handbrake applied, the gear lever moved to the neutral position and the engine stopped. If the vehicle is fitted with an automatic gearbox, the gear selector should be moved to the 'P' position, the handbrake applied and then the engine stopped. The detailed instructions for uncoupling a trailer from this point are illustrated in detail in the accompanying pictures.

The trailer parking brake

Below left:

The first stage of uncoupling a semi-trailer is to apply the trailer parking brake. This is usually located on the nearside of the trailer. The brake is a mechanical cable brake, which is operated by a lever and ratchet. The lever shown has to be moved forward and backward. By doing this the ratchet tightens the cable and this applies the brakes on the wheels of the trailer. When the lever cannot be moved any more, the brakes are 'ON'. The parking brake can also be applied as an additional safety brake, for example, when the vehicle is parked overnight or when there is no option but to leave the vehicle on a steep gradient.

Figure 4 left:
Drawbar trailer. Pictorial view of drawbar coupling.

Trailer legs (or wheels)

Top left:
The trailer support legs or wheels have to be lowered now. This is achieved using the handle shown, which has to be unhooked from its place of stowage, and then extended. The driver/operator should wear gloves for obvious reasons.

Top right:
The handle has been extended and is being turned. This action will slowly lower the trailer support wheels.

Bottom left:
When the feet or wheels of the trailer legs are about 1in (2.5cm) from the ground stop winding. The reason for this is that the difference in height between the king pin and the fifth wheel could be in excess of what is required for a good connection when coupling. This is explained in greater detail later in this chapter.

Bottom right:
When the trailer wheels (landing gear) are lowered, then store the handle in its place of stowage.

Braking and electrical connections

The next stage in the sequence of uncoupling is to release (disconnect) the brake and electrical connections from the semi-trailer. The braking connections are known as air lines. These are internationally colour coded (red, blue and yellow). Most units today have two lines (yellow and red). The purpose of these air lines is to supply compressed air to the semi-trailer from the tractor unit. This enables the brakes on the semi-trailer to operate in unison with those on the tractor unit. The black line is the electrical connection from the tractor unit to the semi-trailer. This line supplies the semi-trailer with the electricity to illuminate the rear lights, stop lamps, indicators and number plate. To avoid danger from passing traffic, it is safer for the driver to undertake the task either from a platform, if fitted between the tractor and trailer, or from the near-side. This vehicle has two air lines — red and yellow — the lighter coloured line being the yellow one.

Left:
It is of the utmost importance that the air taps on the tractor unit are turned off, otherwise air will be lost. Some units are not fitted with air taps and, as an alter-native, non-return valves are provided. Air pressure is immediately shut off automatically as the air line is disconnected. The pressure is restored once the air line is reconnected.

Top left:
The driver has turned the taps to the 'off' position.

Top right:
After the air taps have been turned off, the air lines and black electrical line have to be disconnected from the semi-trailer. This unit has two air lines and one electrical.

Bottom left:
Most articulated vehicles in the UK are fitted with standard male/female connectors. This eliminates the possibility of making wrong connections. It is best to disconnect the air line nearest to you first, and attach it to the appropriate connection on the tractor unit. This will assist in preventing the lines from becoming tangled — an all too common occurrence.

Bottom right:
When an air line has been disconnected from the semi-trailer, attach the line to its appropriate stowage connector on the tractor unit.

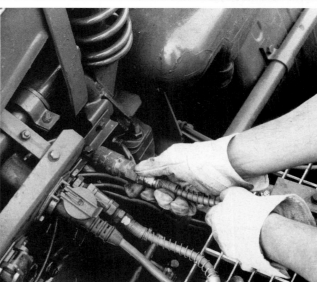

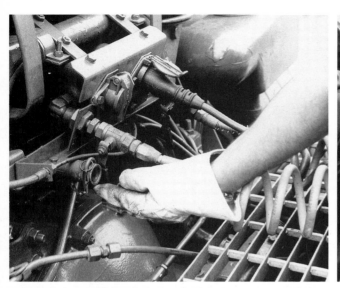

Far left:
On this connector, there is a safety clip which has to be removed before the air line can be stowed.

Left:
The last line to be disconnected is the black — the electrical connection.

Bottom:
The line is stowed into a socket. Note the safety clip on the yellow line, which is in the foreground of the picture.

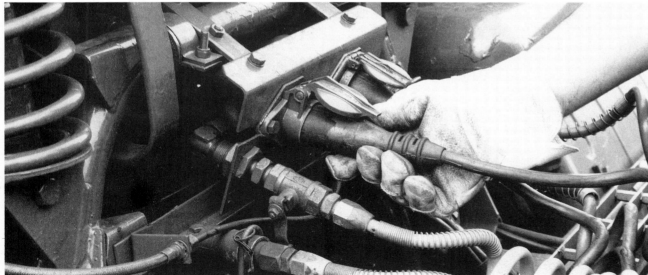

Locking bar and safety catch

Top left:
The locking bar and safety catch are on the offside of the tractor unit. The driver must be aware of any approaching traffic, and let it pass before handling the locking bar. The safety catch illustrated here is in its correct position.

Top right:
Release the safety catch as shown.

Bottom:
When the locking bar is pulled, the king pin on the semi-trailer is unlocked. This disconnects the semi-trailer from the fifth wheel (turntable) on the tractor unit.

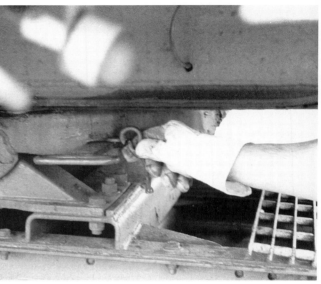

Left:
When all connections to the semi-trailer have been disconnected, the tractor unit should be moved slowly forward away from the semi-trailer. The driver must now check the trailer brake again. The reason for this is that, when the air lines are disconnected, the air brakes on the trailer should come on automatically. If wheel chocks are available, use them.

Below:
The last thing a driver must do before leaving the semi-trailer is to remove the number plate, and put it in the cab.

Bottom left:
The fifth wheel (turntable) can be seen in the middle of the tractor unit. The king pin under the trailer has to be in the centre of the fifth wheel for the locking mechanism to engage. When the king pin locks into the fifth wheel, there should be a positive 'clonk', as the locking bar engages. Nothing must be taken for granted, as complacency has been proved to be a killer. A novice driver must be supervised by a competent instructor when uncoupling and recoupling takes place.

Top right:
The king pin can be seen protruding from beneath the trailer. It is this pin that engages and locks into the fifth wheel on the unit. Note the correct height of the trailer in relation to the fifth wheel on the tractor unit.

Bottom right:
Concentration, observation and vehicle control are essential in order to achieve a safe and correct recoupling of any vehicle.

Recoupling

As with uncoupling, there are numerous factors that have to be considered before recoupling the tractor unit to the trailer. For example, is the trailer too high or too low for the king pin on the trailer to engage correctly with the fifth wheel on the tractor unit? Incorrect height and/or alignment of the king pin can damage the fifth wheel. Alternatively, a false coupling could take place, which is potentially dangerous. It is, therefore, vitally important that all drivers master the art of recoupling since they may not give themselves, or other people, a second chance should the unit disengage whilst on the move. Again the exact procedure for recoupling tractor unit to trailer is explained in the photographic sequence.

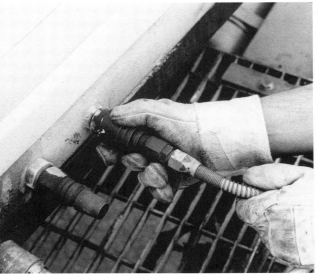

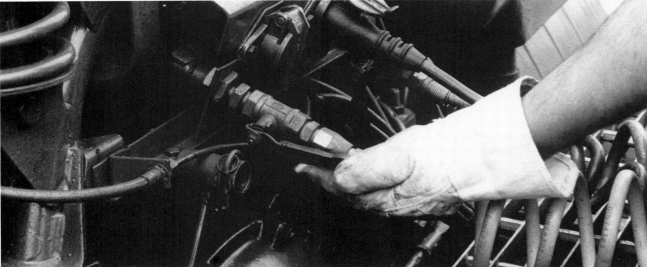

Top left:

The king pin is about to engage on to the fifth wheel. When the pin is correctly engaged with the fifth wheel, the locking bar seen to the left of the fifth wheel will retract. This will have the effect of locking the king pin to the fifth wheel. When recoupling has taken place, the driver must then make numerous safety checks. The first can only be accomplished by selecting first gear and, with the tractor unit handbrake off, trying to drive slowly forward and, in doing so, trying to pull the trailer forward. It must be borne in mind that the trailer brake is still applied (on) and will, as a result, resist any movement. The purpose of this safety check is to make sure there is no false coupling between the tractor unit and trailer. When the driver is sure the unit is coupled, the handbrake of the tractor unit must be applied and neutral selected (or 'P' for vehicles fitted with automatic transmission), and then the engine stopped. The driver must now make sure the locking bar is in the correct position. If it is, the safety catch can be attached to the locking bar.

Top right:

Reconnect the electrical and air lines to the semi-trailer.

Left:

When the air lines have been reconnected, the air taps on the tractor unit must be turned on.

Right:

When all connections have been made, the number plate should be attached to the trailer. The driver should then seek assistance to check all the lights work.

Below right:

The trailer parking brake can then be released, and any wheel chocks removed and stored in the cab. The final checks must now be carried out. Make sure the air pressure is correct; this is achieved by looking at the air pressure gauge. The air pressure could be down after connecting the air line to the semi-trailer. Should the pressure gauge not show the required safe reading, the engine must be started to build up the air pressure to the required level. This must be done before the handbrake is released. Another check, which must be carried out, is for air leaks. The driver should seek assistance to check that there are no air leaks on the air lines. A leak will be detected by a hissing sound. If a hissing sound is heard, the engine should be stopped and the vehicle must not be moved until the fault is rectified. If no fault is found the trailer legs should be raised and the winding handle stored in its appropriate place. After this, the driver can, when safe to do so, move off and carry out a brake test.

6 At the LGV driving test centre

On the day of your test allow adequate time for travelling to the test centre, so that you arrive well before the time stated on your LGV test appointment card. Tests are arranged to a strict timetable therefore, if you arrive later than your appointed time, there might not be adequate time left for the examiner to conduct your test. As a result you are likely to lose your appointment and there is no refund on the fee. When you arrive at the test centre, follow the instructions given as to where to park. When you have parked your vehicle it is the your responsibility to check that all doors and, if fitted, dropsides and tailboard, as well as any equipment carried, are properly secured. In the case of an articulated vehicle or draw-bar outfit, the candidate should also check that the trailer brake lines and lighting leads are properly connected, that the lights work and that the semi-trailer parking brake is not on. In the case of tilt-cab vehicles, the candidate should also ensure that the cab-locking mechanism is secure as the examiner will verify this after the reversing exercise. These checks must be made before going to the waiting room.

When these checks have been made you should then go to the waiting room and wait for the examiner to greet you. This should be at the time as stated on your appointment card. He/she will call out your name and then ask you to sign your name on the form DLV34 (attendance sheet). It is at this point that the test begins. There is no reason why you should not sign the form but, if you refuse to do so, the test may not be conducted. After you have signed your name, the examiner will ask to see your driving licence. If the licence cannot be shown, you will be asked to produce some other evidence of identity that has your signature on it. The signature will then be compared with the one on the form DLV34. This check is to detect any attempt at impersonation.

The acceptable forms of identity specified in the regulations are:
- a signed driving licence issued in Great Britain, Northern Ireland, the Channel Islands, the Isle of Man and other EC member states;
- a signed driving licence issued in a country whose licences may be exchanged for GB licences (these are listed in section B3 of the form D100 which can be obtained from most Post Offices);
- other foreign licences provided they bear the holder's name in the roman alphabet, photograph and signature;
- a signed British Forces licence or a signed driving permit issued by a visiting force;
- a signed international driving permit;
- a signed passport or an identity card issued by the candidate's employer bearing the holder's name in the roman alphabet, photograph and signature.

If a candidate produces an unsigned licence and possesses no other means of confirming his/her identity then the test will, in all probability, not be conducted and the candidate will not normally be offered any vacant slot the same day. The regulations, however, give an examiner discretion in these circumstances. That discretion must be exercised reasonably taking into account the circumstances of the particular case. When the signatures have been compared and found to be acceptable, the examiner will ask you to lead the way to your vehicle. Unlike the basic 'L' test, the LGV driving test does not include an eyesight test, as this was done when you had your medical examination.

7 The reversing exercise

If you are being tested on a category C vehicle the examiner will ask you to bring the vehicle to the edge of the manoeuvring area. This is the starting position for the reversing exercise. You should then make the vehicle safe, stop the engine and get out of the cab to join the examiner. You will now have the exercise clearly explained to you with the aid of a diagram (see figure 4) to describe the requirements and giving precise directions as to the course to be followed. It will also be explained that you should not touch any of the marker cones or cross the yellow boundary lines during the exercise.

The examiner will ask you to drive the vehicle forwards and backwards and, whilst driving the vehicle backwards, steer along a predetermined course, enter a narrow opening and bring it to rest in a predetermined position. The measurements for this exercise are: the distance from the base line Z to cone B should be three times the length of the vehicle used for the test; and that from cone B to cones A and A1 should be twice the length of the vehicle. In the case of vehicles with trailers, cone A1 should be set one yard in from the boundary line. In the case of rigid vehicles without trailers, cone A1 should be set on the boundary line. Exceptionally at centres where there is a safety barrier or other obstruction close to the boundary line and the rigid vehicle used for the test has a large front overhang or limited steering lock, which may make it difficult to negotiate cone B, then cone A1 should be set one yard in from the line.

The distance between cones A and A1 should always be one and a half times the width of the vehicle used for the test and cone B should always be in line with cone A. See figure 5. This exercise is designed to test the candidate's accuracy in manoeuvring the vehicle when reversing. The degree of accuracy required is the ability to occupy a bay one and a half times the width of the vehicle and with the rear of the vehicle within the 3ft stopping area. All round observation should be maintained during the exercise.

During the reversing exercise, the examiner moves from one vantage point to another in order to verify the candidate's handling of this manoeuvre. The examiner will also be looking to see whether the stop lamps are working or damaged, or if there are

The reversing exercise.

Figure 5 right:

The cones are laid out in this diagram for an articulated vehicle in categories C or E.

The reversing exercise commences with the front of the candidate's vehicle in line with the marker cones 'A' and 'A1'. The candidate reverses into the bay, keeping marker 'B' on the offside, and stops with the extreme rear of his vehicle within the 3ft stopping area.

Distances:
'A'-'A1' =
1.5 times width of vehicle
'A'-'B' =
twice length of vehicle
B-Line Z =
three times length of vehicle

Width of bay = 1.5 times width of vehicle

At the discretion of the examiner, the bay can be set in the following way:
a) The same length as the vehicle used for the test;
b) Three feet longer;
c) Three feet shorter;
d) six feet shorter.

● **indicates 18in marker cone**
◖ **indicates 18in marker cone with 5ft coloured pole.**

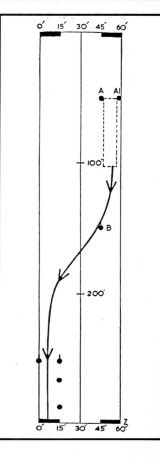

LENGTH OF VEHICLE		CONE A	CONE B
METRES	FEET		
4.5	15	225	255
4.8	16	220	252
5.1	17	215	249
5.4	18	210	246
5.7	19	205	243
6.0	20	200	240
6.4	21	195	237
6.7	22	190	234
7.0	23	185	231
7.3	24	180	228
7.6	25	175	225
7.9	26	170	222
8.2	27	165	219
8.5	28	160	216
8.8	29	155	213
9.1	30	150	210
9.4	31	145	207
9.7	32	140	204
10.0	33	135	201
10.3	34	130	198
10.6	35	125	195
10.9	36	120	192
11.2	37	115	189
11.5	38	110	186
11.8	39	105	183
12.1	40	100	180
12.5	41	95	177
12.8	42	90	174
13.1	43	85	171
13.4	44	80	168
13.7	45	75	165
14.0	46	70	162
14.3	47	65	159
14.6	48	60	156
14.9	49	55	153
15.2	50	50	150
15.5	51	45	147
15.8	52	40	144
16.1	53	35	141
16.4	54	30	138
16.7	55	25	135
17.0	56	20	132
17.3	57	15	129
17.6	58	10	126
17.9	59	5	123
18.2	60	0	120

Left:
The reversing area has a permanent ready reckoner marked on the road surface. This is used by the examiners as a guide to cone positioning. At LGV test centres, the guide lines go from one side of the boundary across to the other. This is a picture of the training area at the DSA Cardington Training Establishment.

Far left:
Reversing exercise measurements: ready reckoner for the position of cones.

When a candidate is being tested on an articulated vehicle or one drawing a trailer, his/her knowledge of uncoupling and re-coupling the semi or drawn trailer safely will be tested orally. About six questions will be asked as appropriate, on the correct sequence of operation and the safety factors involved.

Below:
The candidate has been asked a question relating to the air lines.

Right:
After the questions, the examiner will explain the reversing exercise, making full use of the diagram to describe the requirements.

any other aspects of the vehicle's condition which might raise doubts as to whether it is in a roadworthy condition or not. This examination also includes ensuring that all 'L' plates are present. If a lamp failure is evident during the exercise, it will be brought to the candidate's attention. If time permits, the candidate should be given a chance to rectify the fault. However, if it is not possible to effect a repair, then the test will be terminated as the law requires the vehicle to be in good and efficient working order whenever it is used on the road.

Another important aspect regarding the reversing exercise is that, whilst the exercise should be completed, whenever possible, in one manoeuvre but, if a single 'shunting' manoeuvre proves necessary, the candidate should not drive further forward than the boundary of the area marked by cones A and A1, and should not take more than two 'shunts' throughout the exercise. After the reversing exercise has been satisfactorily completed, the examiner will get into the cab and, in the case of a tilt-cab vehicle, will ask if the candidate is satisfied that the cab-locking mechanism is secure, and how does he/she know it is. The candidate should answer that the cab is secure (**make sure that the cab *is* secure before going into the waiting room**), and no warning light is showing. The latter check cannot be relied on as there could be a

faulty lamp in the warning panel. If seat belts are fitted, they should be worn. The examiner will then ask you to drive forward when you're ready. You will now drive to another part of the test centre where you will undertake the braking exercise. The braking exercise must be carried out within the test centre prior to heading out on to the public highway.

The pictures on pp34-37 show a real 'on the job' reversing manoeuvre. These illustrate that it is of the utmost importance that a driving test candidate is able to reverse an LGV with accuracy and control. For example, when a driver of an LGV makes deliveries or collections from company depots each day, there may not be adequate space to manoeuvre safely up to or into a loading bay without a couple of 'shunts'. Unlike the comparative safety of the manoeuvring area at a test centre, there is considerable potential for accidents in these circumstances — accidents which could easily be avoided. In order to comply with existing Health & Safety legislation, any responsible company will have staff — known as bankmen — trained to assist drivers to carry out the more awkward manoeuvres. Organisations such as RoSPA (the Royal Society for the Prevention of Accidents) provide training courses for these staff members. Successful completion of the course is recognised by the award of a Certificate of Competence.

Bottom left:
This is the view of the start of the reversing exercise as it is approached. Note the 4in wide boundary line (yellow) and marker cones at the edge of the boundary area. All the following photographs were taken by the author at the Training Establishment of the DSA and are not of an actual LGV test, since the recording of the latter could have led to possible interference in the candidate's concentration.

Left:
When the examiner directs you to move the vehicle up to cones A and A1, you should take the usual precautions of making sure that the handbrake is applied and the gear lever/selector is in neutral before starting the engine. Then, when safe to do so, move the vehicle forward, keeping close to (but do not touch or pass) Cone A. The reason for this is that you will need all the space on the nearside of your vehicle that is available to you for the exercise. Note that Cones A and B are in line.

Right:
This candidate has stopped the vehicle in the correct position to start the exercise. It should be remembered that this exercise is designed to test your accuracy and control in manoeuvring the vehicle when reversing. The degree of accuracy required is your ability to occupy a bay one and a half times the width of the vehicle and with the rear of the vehicle within the 3ft stopping area. The bay can be seen in the background. All round observation should be maintained during the exercise.

Far left:
Before starting the exercise take all round observation before moving. Do not turn the steering wheel while stationary. This would be marked by the examiner as a control fault.

Left:
Move the vehicle as slowly as possible and, at the same time, turn the steering wheel quickly to the left. Note that the candidate is using the left mirror. This enables the candidate to monitor the trailer and check its angle of travel.

Below left:
Remember that you should not cross the yellow boundary line with the full width of a tyre, nor should you displace any marker cones (as illustrated earlier) with any part of the vehicle. Note how this candidate is looking at the rear tractor wheel in relation to its position to the boundary line.

Right:
The left steering lock is progressively reduced. Cone B is about to come into the candidate's view.

Far right:
The candidate is now reversing in a straight line and heading for the bay that can be seen. Note that the candidate is using the nearside mirror, and that the examiner is observing the candidate's performance by moving from one vantage point to another while the exercise is being performed.

Bottom:
Note how the candidate is steering slightly to the right. This action places the rear of the trailer on course for the bay.

Top left:
Do not touch any cone when entering the box. The right steering lock is being taken off, as the trailer is on course in the bay.

Bottom left:
Some test candidates use a guide on the side of the trailer that, when lined up with the edge of the box, indicates to the driver when to stop. The guide is seen here from the off side mirror. This candidate is leaning out of the window in order to check the exact point at which to stop.

Left:
When the vehicle has been brought to rest, the handbrake should be applied and the gear lever/selector placed in neutral. The examiner is checking the position of the extreme rear of the vehicle in relation to the box. The rear of the vehicle should be within the 3ft yellow stopping area which forms part of the reversing bay.

Right:
The driver has arrived at a depot. A loading bay, up to which the driver has to reverse, can be seen on the left. It should always be remembered that the current situation, which seems to be clear in the depot, could change within seconds.

Below right:
The driver has been asked to move forward by a bankman (out of sight in this picture). The bankman will assist the driver to the bay.

Top left:
The bankman is explaining the meaning of the signals that he will give.

Top right:
The bankman is guiding the driver towards the bay.

Bottom left:
When the vehicle is at this angle, the rear of the vehicle cannot be seen by the driver. He, therefore, needs the assistance of a bankman, who is the driver's 'Third Eye', to supplement the information provided by the two mirrors.

Bottom right:
Note how the potentially dangerous situation has arisen in the depot. Another bay has been opened and a driver can be seen alongside a van. The driver of our lorry cannot see this and is, therefore, unaware of the changed position without receiving further information either from his mirrors or from the bankman.

Right:
The bankman is directing the driver to the bay.

Bottom left:
The driver is on course. He is checking progress continually through the use of his mirrors.

Bottom right:
The importance of knowing the length of the vehicle being driven can be seen here. The driver is using the offside mirror to monitor progress.

Far right:
The driver is leaning out of the window to gain every bit of vision that is available to him. This, combined with the assistance of the bankman, will enable the manoeuvre to be completed safely.

8 The braking exercise

Right:
When you have brought the vehicle to rest after this stage of the LGV test, the examiner will show you a diagram (figure 6) of the braking exercise. This candidate is being shown the diagram.

The candidate is required to drive forward and reach a speed of about 20mph by the time the mark (cones A and A1) is reached. The brakes should then be applied to bring the vehicle to a stop as quickly and as safely as possible.

Now that you have seen a true-to-life reversing manoeuvre, let us proceed to the next part of the test. This is the braking exercise. When the examiner has got in the cab he/she will ask you to move off. Before doing so, all round observation must be taken, as it has been known for people to wander around a test centre. You will have to drive across the manoeuvring area as directed by the examiner. After a short distance the examiner will ask you to pull up at a particular place. When the instruction to pull up is given, use the mirrors and stop the vehicle in the place to which you have been directed.

The braking exercise must be carried out on the test centre track, and before leaving the centre. When you have stopped the vehicle you should take the usual precautions to make the vehicle safe. The place at which you have stopped is the starting point for the braking exercise. The examiner will then explain the course to be followed and the mark at which the brakes should be applied. This point will be not less than 200ft from the starting point. The whole exercise will be clearly explained to you. See figure 6.

On the completion of the braking exercise the next phase of the test takes place on the public highway and the examiner will, thus, instruct you to leave the test centre. Remember that he/she will be checking how you handle the exit on to the public highway just as much as any other stage of the test.

STOPPING AREA

A   A1

The braking exercise

Figure 6 far left:
The candidate drives forward over a distance of about 200ft to reach a speed of approximately 20mph. After passing marker cones A and A1 the driver should apply the brakes, stopping the vehicle as quickly and as safely as possible whilst retaining full control.

Left:
When the examiner has explained the course to be followed, you will be asked to move off when you're ready. Remember to take all round observation before releasing the handbrake, then build your speed up to 20mph. As soon as the front bumper is level with cones A and A1 the footbrake should be applied. In good conditions, a well maintained goods vehicle in the hands of a well-trained and competent driver, should stop in the following distances from 20mph:
- **Up to four tons unladen weight: 20ft;**
- **Up to six tons unladen weight: 25ft;**
- **Up to 10 tons unladen weight: 35ft.**

In assessing the candidate's ability to stop, the examiner must take into consideration the surface conditions and the weight of the vehicle.

It should be remembered that, with an empty vehicle, some or all the wheels may lock if excessive brake pedal pressure is applied. In the case of articulated vehicles or drawbar outfits, this may result in jack-knifing, particularly if the drawing vehicle and trailer are out of line when the wheels lock. As a result the examiner will look for correct application of the brakes and use of the steering when assessing this exercise. Make sure that the vehicle you use for the test has good brakes. If you can't stop within a reasonable distance when carrying out this exercise, the examiner may decide to terminate the test there and then in the interests of public safety; in which case you will lose your test fee.

When the vehicle has been brought to rest, apply the handbrake and select neutral gear. You are now going to do the main body of the test on the road.

9 The gear changing exercise

Shortly after leaving the test centre, the examiner will ask you to 'pull up on the left at a convenient place' or 'pull up along here'. The purpose of the request is to prepare you for the start of the third exercise of the test — the gear changing exercise. When you have brought the vehicle to rest, apply the handbrake and move the gear lever/selector to neutral. The examiner will then ask you to move off in the lowest gear and change up through the gears, using each gear in turn until you reach third or fourth gear. After completing this sequence of gear changes you will be requested to change down using each gear in turn until the lowest gear has been selected. In vehicles that have splitter boxes and two-speed axles, you should be told that it is only necessary to use the normal range. You may use the footbrake to adjust vehicle speed before selecting the next lower gear. The purpose of this exercise is to test your ability to use the lower gears. The examiner will be looking for a smooth engagement and progressive use of each gear. When you have selected the lowest gear at the conclusion of the exercise, the examiner will ask you to drive on. It must be remembered that the vehicle is not stationary and, therefore, you will be doing a rolling moving off. The mirrors must be used and, if traffic is seen waiting to overtake you, but cannot because of approaching traffic, you must decide either to signal your intention to move off or to pull up on the left. The prevailing circumstances at the time will dictate what action you should take.

Due to its weight, a large goods vehicle requires rather more gear ratios than a car to ensure optimum performance over a wide range of speeds and conditions. This is achieved in a number of ways; for example, the vehicle may have a splitter, range-change gearbox or a two-speed rear axle.

The necessity of a gearbox

The object of the gearbox is to enable the engine's speed and turning effort (torque) to be adjusted relative to the vehicle's road speed so that it responds to the requirements of the various road and traffic conditions. Good anticipation is often required to ensure that the driver is in the most appropriate gear for each situation as it arises.

Where heavy loads are being hauled, the power-to-weight ratio is low, and if the gear ratio steps are too large engine speed will drop to such an extent during gear changes that it becomes impossible to maintain momentum. Therefore to minimise engine speed fall-off whilst changing gears; smaller gear ratio steps are required, that is, more ratios are necessary to respond to slight changes in vehicle load and road conditions. The usual way to extend the number of gear ratios is to utilise a two-speed auxiliary gearbox in a series with a three, four, five or six-speed main gearbox, thereby doubling the number of gear ratios available. With a three, four, five or six-speed gearbox, the gear ratios are thereby increased to six, eight, 10 or 12 respectively.

Splitters

A splitter gives a second set of ratios between the ratios of the main gearbox, thereby halving the ratio steps. Normally achieved by a button or other switch on the gear lever, the gear shift pattern of 1st low, 1st high, 2nd low, 2nd high, 3rd low and so on is adopted. The driver selects the low and high ratio gears as and when required. When running lightly-laden it is not always necessary to use every individual step. However the splitter often comes into its own when gentle gradients are encountered on motorways; good anticipation by the driver enables a half-shift down to be made in good time to prevent speed dropping off too much and can even obviate the need for a full downshift.

Range change

In contrast to the splitter, the range change gives two completely separate ranges of ratios. The auxiliary two-speed gearbox will have one direct-drive ratio and the other is equal to just over half the gear ratio spread from bottom to top. In other words, with a four-speed gearbox and range change the driver will start off in first gear, low range, and progress to fourth gear before changing the range and using the main gearbox ratios, in high range, to give fifth to eighth gears. The change of range is sometimes achieved by a switch — in which case the driver moves the lever back to the first gear position for fifth gear — and sometimes by moving the

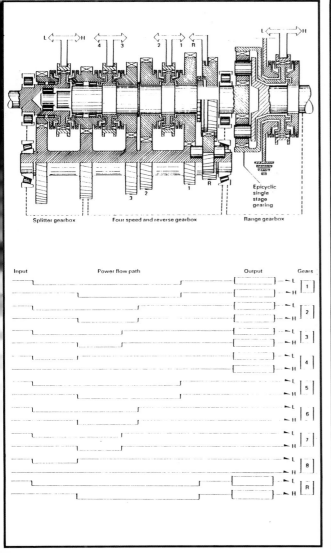

Splitter gearbox   **Four speed and reverse gearbox**   **Range gearbox**

Epicyclic single stage gearing

Input	Power flow path	Output	Gears	
			L	1
			H	
			L	2
			H	
			L	3
			H	
			L	4
			H	
			L	5
			H	
			L	6
			H	
			L	7
			H	
			L	8
			H	
			L	R
			H	

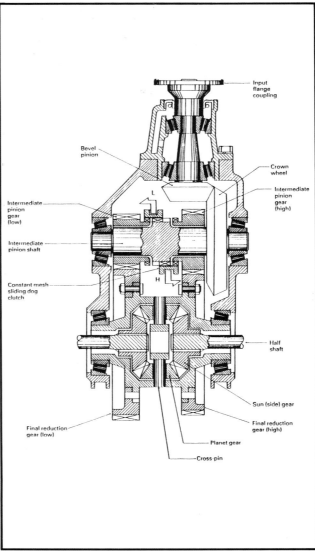

Input flange coupling

Bevel pinion

Crown wheel

Intermediate pinion gear (high)

Intermediate pinion gear (low)

Intermediate pinion shaft

Constant mesh sliding dog clutch

Half shaft

Sun (side) gear

Final reduction gear (high)

Final reduction gear (low)

Planet gear

Cross-pin

Figure 7 far left:
16 speed synchromesh with range change and integral splitter gears.

Figure 8 left:
Two speed double reduction helical gear axle.

gear lever across a gate, against spring pressure, and then continuing the sequence in a separate gate.

Two-speed axles

Sometimes the spread of ratios is achieved not by an auxiliary gearbox but by a two-speed axle, in which the gear reduction can be chosen to provide a high cruising speed on good roads, or a lower top speed but better climbing ability in hilly country or for off-road use.

Therefore, to enable the vehicle to operate effectively under either motorway speeds, start/stop work in towns and accelerating in conditions without overloading or driving at excessive speeds, and without having to have an eight, 10 or 12-speed gearbox, a two-speed gear reduction may be built into the final drive axle.

Combining a high and low ratio in the same axle doubles the number of gears available from a standard gearbox. The low range of gears will then provide the maximum pulling power for heavy duty operations on unmade roads, whereas the high range of gears allows maximum speed when conditions are favourable. From the wide range of gear ratios the driver can choose the exact combination to suit most conditions of load and type of road so that the engine will always operate at peak efficiency and near to its maximum torque speed.

Synchromesh or constant-mesh?

These days the car driver takes synchromesh for granted. This automatically adjusts the relative speed of the gears within the gearbox as gear changes are made, enabling silent gear changes to be made each time. This has the drawback of increasing the weight of the change; on a car this is usually well within acceptable limits, but on a large vehicle it can make the gear change unacceptably heavy and for that that reason it is not a universal fitting. On vehicles without synchromesh a constant-mesh gearbox is fitted, which takes some skill on behalf of the driver to achieve silent changes. Double-declutching is then needed; on upward changes the driver releases the clutch in neutral, and then depresses it again to move to the next gear once engine revs have dropped to the right speed to engage the next gear. Going down the box, the same declutching process is used but the accelerator has to be used to increase engine speed to the correct level for the lower gear. At the other end of the spectrum sophisticated electronics are now used by some manufacturers to operate the gearbox and make it easier for the driver.

Below:
If traffic can be seen in the mirrors waiting to overtake you but is unable to do so due to oncoming traffic, then, if the road ahead is clear, signal your intention to move off by the use of the direction indicator and continue normal driving.

10 Stopping normally

Below left:

If any other road user can be seen in the mirrors, a signal of your intention to pull in and stop must be given.

Below:

If the examiner requests you to pull up just after the next road on the left, the mirrors must be used and, if following traffic can be seen, an arm signal should be given. This informs other road users of your intention to slow down or stop.

During the test, the examiner will ask you to 'pull up' on the left on several occasions. The reason for this is to see if you can pull up safely on the left whilst in traffic. You could be asked to pull up just before the next road on the left or just after the next road on the left. Should a direction indicator signal be used at the wrong time and place, it could result in failure. If the examiner requests you to pull up on the left, providing there is no side road on the immediate left, the mirrors must be used and, if following traffic can be seen,

an 'I intend to move in to the left' direction indicator signal should be used. If the instruction to 'pull up' on the left requires you to stop immediately after a road junction, you should check in the mirrors to ascertain the position of any following traffic and, once the junction has been passed, use the direction indicators to warn any following traffic of your intended manoeuvre. Use of the indicator prior to the junction could confuse other road users into thinking that you were intending to turn left at the junction.

Left:
**Alternatively, a direction
indicator signal should be
used. This also informs
following drivers of your
intention to move in and stop
on the left. The signal should
be given when you are level
with the junction on the left
and not before.**

11 Moving off

The prime consideration when moving off is that you do so safely and smoothly showing awareness of the presence of other road users, including pedestrians. The moving off test will also examine your ability to start off from an uphill or downhill gradient, and from a position behind a stationary vehicle. All the moving off manoeuvres must be accomplished safely and smoothly. Remember, when moving off, that the examiner will also still be watching for your use of the mirrors and direction indicators.

Left:
If the examiner requests you to pull up just before the next road on the left, the mirrors must be used and if following traffic is seen, an arm signal to show your intention to slow down and stop must be given. It should always be remembered that a signal of intent, by arm or direction indicator, should be given if it will inform any other road user, including pedestrians, of your intention to slow down or change direction. The use of signals will be assessed throughout the test by the examiner. The examiner will be watching the use of signals carefully in order to check whether they are necessary, appropriate and given in good time and at the right place. You should also remember to cancel any direction indicator after use, as this is also closely monitored.

Right:
While preparing to move off, the candidate has noticed another driver about to emerge from the left. Consequently, he/she has no option but to wait.

Below right:
A pedestrian has left a house and is about to cross the road in front of you. She is checking to make sure it is safe to do so. You should, therefore, allow the pedestrian to cross the road before moving off.

Far right:
When the road ahead can be seen to be clear the mirrors must be used to check the position of any traffic behind. If traffic can be seen about to overtake you, wait until it has passed then check the nearside mirror.

Top left:
If pedestrians can be seen in the mirror — as in this situation — wait until they have passed. Children can also be seen on the pavement. These are about to pass your vehicle, and you must be aware of the potential dangers from this situation.

Left:
When the pedestrians have passed the vehicle look in the offside mirror again; if no traffic is near, check the nearside mirror again and, if no potential danger can be seen, look over your right shoulder.

Bottom left:
You must always look over your right shoulder before moving off from the kerb. This is to make sure that the road behind you is clear of any other road user that might not be seen in the mirror.

Right:
If the road ahead and to the rear can be seen to be clear, there is no need to signal as it will be of no use to anyone.

Moving off on a gradient

Below right:
Apart from the proper use of the mirrors, the correct co-ordination of the accelerator, clutch and handbrake must be accomplished, so that a smooth move off from the kerb is achieved.

Moving off at an angle

Top left:
During the test the examiner will ask you to pull up on the left just before you get to the next stationary vehicle and leave enough room to move away. Like any other time when you have to reduce speed, the mirrors must be used and, if any traffic is following, a direction indicator or hand signal to inform other road users of your intention to move in to the left and slow down or stop must be given. If no other road user is seen, a signal is unnecessary.

Top right:
You must allow adequate clearance from the vehicle in front in order to be able to move away safely. The driver of this vehicle has allowed sufficient room to be able to move off. In all probability you will have to use the other side of the road to enable you to move away, as you will need to have a good margin of safety between the vehicle being driven and the stationary vehicle.

Bottom:
Make sure the trailer is well clear of the stationary vehicle before you straighten up and resume the normal driving position.

12 Hazard recognition and planning

Recapping slightly, in Chapter 1 we discussed the perceptual skills involved in driving vehicles — the combination of observation, identification and prediction. However, without proper concentration from the driver, observation in itself is meaningless. Perception comes from observing, seeing and assessing, formulating a safe driving plan, recognising hazards in good time, and thus acting on the information seen well before the hazard is reached. The driver needs to be able to recognise and understand a given situation in good time, searching, identifying, predicting, and being able to use the appropriate controls smoothly as and when the circumstances to do so arise. Some drivers do not look well ahead and are forced to react hurriedly when a problem arises. Often, in these circum-

stances, immediate reactions mean that control of the vehicle is impaired, leading, in certain weather conditions, to the jack-knifing of the trailer, for example, with potential injury to both LGV driver and other road users. Remember to keep alert all the time you are behind the wheel.

The examiner will be watching to see if you take appropriate action in good time for a particular hazard — keeping the vehicle under control, in the appropriate gear, and unhurried in your movements. Late and sudden braking or gear changing show a lack of foresight and planning. The following examples show situations that can occur at any time and place.

Top left:

This dangerous situation has occurred because the LGV driver ignored the presence of the car waiting to emerge. At the same time, the driver has not taken the length of his vehicle into consideration before starting to turn. If the driver of the LGV does not look over his right shoulder to check the position of the trailer, an accident will occur. The use of the offside mirror, while the LGV is at its present angle, would not show the driver the dangerous situation he has caused.

Top right:

If the driver looks over his right shoulder while turning, as this driver is doing, he will see the position of the trailer. He will, therefore, have time to pull up before a collision occurs.

Bottom:

Although half the road is obstructed with a 'Fun Fair' it is still open to two-way traffic. Consequently, opposing traffic could appear at any time. This, combined with a pedestrian in your path of travel, should make the driver realise the potential danger. Thus the mirrors must be used and a reduction in speed made.

Right:

Road works obstruct the driver's side of the road on the approach to a roundabout. An oncoming vehicle is seen leaving the roundabout. Since the driver's side of the road is obstructed, he should not cross the hazard lines unless he can see that the road is clear well ahead. As the road ahead is not clear, the driver should give way to the approaching vehicle in accordance with the *Highway Code*.

Below right:

A stationary car transporter can be seen on a bend ahead; the loading ramps are down and it is possible that new vehicles are being delivered to a garage. As the hazard is on a bend, there is no option but to use the mirrors and reduce speed. In doing so the driver will have adequate time to pull up if necessary or proceed as the situation demands.

Left:

When approaching a level crossing and amber lights start to flash, the mirrors must be used and, if following traffic is seen, an arm signal to show the driver's intention to slow down and stop should be given. This signal will be reinforced when the brakes are applied, since the brake light signals will then also be shown.

Below left:

By looking well ahead any potential danger should be seen in good time. As soon as the horseriders are seen, the mirrors must be used and, if appropriate, an arm signal to inform other road users and horseriders that you are about to reduce speed must be given. The speed reduction must be achieved well before reaching the hazard, otherwise the size of your vehicle and noise from your engine could, in this case, scare the animals. Show courtesy and consideration for other road users, and comply with the *Highway Code*.

Right:

Should you join a road and be confronted with a situation like this — where it is obvious a delivery is taking place — you have no option but to be patient and wait until the driver of the delivery vehicle returns, as there is inadequate room to pass the obstruction. If you decide to drive on the footpath to pass the stationary vehicle, remember the advice section 50 in the *Highway Code* gives. If you do not know, do not be surprised if you fail the test.

Below right:

There are times when road works are in progress. By looking well ahead the driver will be able to formulate a safe driving plan. Due to the length of the vehicle, and the small amount of road space available, especially when turning right, this hazard is difficult to negotiate. It is, therefore, of the utmost importance that the mirrors are used, that a signal of your intention is given, that the correct course for the hazard is adopted and that speed is reduced. All this must be accomplished in good time.

Top left:

This and the next four photographs are a sequence showing how to handle the approach to road works. Warning signs combined with cones warn of extensive road works ahead. Consequently, the mirrors must be used and a reduction of speed made. As speed is reduced so a lower gear should be selected.

Top right:

A warning sign, together with what is seen, tells the driver that there is a contraflow ahead. The mirrors must be used again and, if necessary, a further reduction of speed should be made. The driver should take note of the sharp deviation of the road ahead. Correct positioning of the vehicle is imperative.

Bottom:

As the contraflow is about to be entered the offside mirror must be used. This enables the driver to gauge the position of the trailer in relation to the cones.

Right:
It is of the utmost importance that speed is reduced and a low gear selected. The driver should allow enough time to be able to steer the correct course required for this hazard. The driver must ensure that the overhang of the front offside of the vehicle is not allowed to touch the temporary cones in the centre of the road, especially as there is oncoming traffic. The mirrors must be used again.

Below right:
When the front of the vehicle has entered the contraflow, the nearside mirrors must be used so that the position of the trailer can be seen. When the vehicle is on a straight course, the driver must ascertain the condition of the road ahead and formulate a driving plan to deal with the perceived condition of the road ahead.

13 Using the mirrors and the 'cockpit drill'

The correct use of mirrors is an essential element of driving safely. By law vehicles have to be fitted with mirrors to provide a view of the road behind the vehicle and the examiner will be checking the candidate's use of mirrors throughout the test. Prior to the test, therefore, it is of paramount importance that the trainee driver comes to regard the use of mirrors as second nature.

There are two types of mirrors — flat and convex. The flat type of mirror gives a true picture of the road behind. The convex mirror is slightly curved and gives a wider field of vision; at the same time following vehicles seen in this type of mirror seem smaller. Because of this, vehicles look further away then they really are and this can be potentially dangerous unless the driver is wholly confident in the use of the mirrors. Most LGVs are fitted with the flat type of mirror supplemented by additional convex mirrors. Examples of these mirrors are shown in this chapter.

The 'cockpit drill'

Before starting the engine numerous safety checks must be made. They are not only for your own safety but also that of other road users, including pedestrians. The safety check is called the 'cockpit drill'. This ensures that the driver omits no detail and, therefore, leaves nothing to chance. The items to be checked are:

- The doors are properly closed;
- The driving seat is in the correct position so that the driver is able to use the pedals and other controls comfortably;
- The mirrors are properly adjusted;
- The handbrake is on;
- The gear lever/selector is in neutral;
- If seat belts are fitted, use them;
- Adequate fuel is in the tank;
- Air pressure is correct after starting the engine.

Whilst carrying out the safety checks, you might find that it is necessary to alter the position of the driver's seat. If this is required, then it may well also be necessary to readjust the mirrors. The offside mirror(s) can be adjusted by the driver, but you will need assistance from someone to adjust the nearside mirror(s). The mirror(s) should be adjusted so that the side of the vehicle is just visible. Contrary to some advice given, you must move your head to be able to look in the mirror(s) to gain from the information that is seen.

The driver must aim to have the best possible view around the vehicle at all times. This can only be achieved by ensuring that all windows are kept clean inside and out. A vehicle can be fitted with any number of mirrors of all types, shapes and sizes. But these are all useless unless they are kept clean at all times. Keep them clean! Again, it is important to note in the context of the test that the examiner will be looking at the overall condition of the vehicle, and an LGV with dirty windows or poorly positioned mirrors will not create a positive impression.

Below left:
There are three mirrors fitted on the nearside of this vehicle, the lower main (flat) mirror gives a view of the side of the trailer and the road to its nearside. The area of road that cannot be seen in the main mirror is visible through two additional (convex) mirrors. Because of the wide angle of view available in these additional mirrors, an area of road can be seen by a driver that would otherwise be blind to him.

Below:
This is a good example illustrating the use of mirrors when turning left. The main mirror shows any following traffic, whilst the upper convex mirror shows the driver the position of the nearside wheels in relation to the kerb while turning.

14 Turning left at junctions

Most road users will appreciate and understand that one of the most difficult and potentially dangerous manoeuvres is a right turn. This is particularly true at crossroads, because other road users may be entering the junction from other directions. The same potential dangers apply to an LGV driver when turning left, not only because of the size of the vehicle, but the position on the road that has to be adopted to be able to carry out the manoeuvre. Many drivers of smaller vehicles are unaware of the amount of road space that is required for an LGV to turn left and right. Some road users think drivers of LGVs are being selfish when they approach a corner, because in their opinion, too much road is being used and thus it is difficult for the motorist to overtake.

The following sequence of photographs shows the correct and incorrect way for an LGV to turn left. Whilst undertaking the manoeuvre you must always be aware that there are other road users who may be inconsiderate, either through ignorance or by deliberate action, and thus make the turn more difficult.

Right:
The driver of the LGV has positioned his vehicle correctly for a left turn. An experienced car driver has understood the situation and has, therefore, pulled up well away from the stop line. When the traffic signals change, the driver of the car will hold back thus allowing the LGV to move off without hindrance.

Top left:
The inconsiderate driver of this car is trying to pass the LGV. If the driver of the LGV has not looked in the nearside mirror, he will not be aware of the irresponsible action the car driver is taking.

Top right:
The driver has positioned and brought the LGV to rest correctly at a junction for a left turn. The mirrors must be used before the vehicle is moved, for reasons illustrated in the following sequence.

Bottom left:
By being in the correct position on the approach, there is adequate space on the nearside to complete the manoeuvre. The mirrors must still be used so that the driver can check progress and avoid hitting the kerb.

Bottom right:
Although the driver of the LGV has adopted the correct position for a left turn, this action has been ruined by an inconsiderate car driver who has squeezed down the nearside of the LGV.

Right:
The inconsiderate car driver could be in some danger unless the LGV driver is fully aware of the car's presence through the use of the mirrors before commencing the turn.

Far right:
The driver of this LGV has positioned the vehicle too close to the left-hand kerb. It is important to remember that this vehicle is over 50ft in length. The driver should always bear this length in mind — as well as the vehicle's height — when contemplating the route to be followed.

Left:
As a consequence of adopting an incorrect position on the road, commencing the left turn too early and failing to use the mirrors properly, this driver's trailer is about to demolish a street name sign.

Top left:

This sequence of four pictures illustrates the procedure for emerging from a minor to major road at a junction. The road to the right can be seen to be clear.

Top right:

Looking to your left a car can be seen; the driver waves to you to emerge. This apparently helpful gesture should be ignored, unless the LGV driver has independently verified that it is safe to complete the manoeuvre, as circumstances can change rapidly and good intentions on the part of the car driver could lead to potential danger.

Bottom left:

Having ensured that it it is safe to do so, the LGV driver has accepted the invitation of the approaching driver to emerge, and has started to undertake the manoeuvre. Note how much road space is being used to enter the junction.

Bottom right:

The car driver was not aware of the amount of road the LGV would require to complete the turn and has, therefore, moved forward. In consequence the driver of the LGV cannot complete the manoeuvre. The LGV is, as a result, blocking the road. A helpful gesture from another road user is not always the benefit it initially appears to be.

Left:

If you have to cross a cycle, bus or tram lane to turn left, the correct position on the approach should be adopted, and the mirrors must be used. You should not straddle the lane on the nearside.

Below left:

Signal your intention to turn left in good time.

Right:
Lose any unwanted speed in good time, then select the appropriate gear for the turn, well before reaching the junction.

Top left:

You must look in the mirrors again before you start the turn. If any other road user is seen on your left (nearside mirror[s]) give way to them, then when safe to do so you can cross the designated lane. The offside mirror must also be used to look at the overhang of your vehicle, as another road user could be passing too close. In this cir-cumstance the other road user could possibly collide with the rear offside overhang of your vehicle as you turn the corner.

Bottom left:

This is another good example of using the mirrors. A poten-tial danger, which might not be seen in one mirror because of the angle of the vehicle while turning a corner, can be seen in another.

Left:

The importance of using the mirrors can never be overes-timated. As an example, when turning left use the nearside mirrors; in doing so you will be able to check the direction of travel the trailer is taking in relation to the kerb, and be aware of any pedestrian who could be waiting to cross the road.

Below:

It is essential to look in the mirrors, so that you are aware of the presence and position of any following traffic. A direction signal should then be given before changing course and slowing down.

Below right:

The correct road position for turning at a junction is of the utmost importance. The driver of this LGV is in the correct position on the road for this type of vehicle for turning right at a T-junction.

15 Turning right at junctions

There are numerous potential dangers that can be created, either by the LGV driver or another road user, when turning right. We discussed the problems associated with lack of planning and taking a situation for granted in Chapter 12 and the importance of correct planning and traffic awareness cannot be overstated in this manoeuvre. There are few manoeuvres more critical for the LGV driver than the right turn across traffic and, thus, the use of the correct approach and vehicle handling is essential. The accompanying photographs explore in detail the techniques that should be adopted in undertaking a right turn.

Top left:
Even though the driver of the LGV is in the correct position for turning right, with the right signal of intent operating, an impatient/inconsiderate driver cannot wait for the LGV to complete the right turn. The car in this picture appeared whilst the photograph was being taken. Consequently, the resulting photograph was entirely unposed and illustrates graphically the importance of good road sense.

Top right:
The driver of the LGV has omitted to signal his intention to turn right. As a result, the driver of the car is not aware of the course the LGV is about to take.

Bottom:
This LGV was in the correct position for turning right, and is half way through the manoeuvre.

Right:
This photograph shows how much road is being used when an LGV turns right. Note the presence of stationary vehicles. This makes the approach to the junction more awkward for the LGV driver.

Top left:

When approaching a T-junction from a side road, there could be numerous hazards that have to be negotiated before the junction is reached. This illustration and the next two are a sequence. The driver is proceeding down a side road that has numerous stationary vehicles. The driver of the LGV has been asked by the examiner to 'Take the next road on the right'. The next road on the right is a T-junction at a major road. The mirrors have been used and a direction indicator signal of his intention to turn right is now being used. The correct course to steer the LGV through the hazards is being accomplished.

Top right:

The mirrors have been used again, and speed is being reduced by proper use of the brakes.

Bottom left:

On reaching the junction the vehicle is stopped and the handbrake is applied. Note the correct position of the vehicle while waiting to turn.

Bottom right:

Remember what can go wrong if you do not plan ahead.

One-way streets

Right:

When in a one-way street, be guided by road markings. Use the mirrors and, if turning left or right, signal your intention and, if safe to do so, enter the appropriate lane for your intended direction of travel.

Below right:

Be careful when leaving a one-way street, as you could be joining a road that has two-way traffic.

Whenever you leave a hazard of any type, the mirrors (offside and nearside) should be used. By checking in the mirrors you will be aware of the traffic and its position behind you.

16 Roundabouts

Roundabouts are designed to improve traffic flow at busy or complex road junctions. They should be well signposted in advance with guidance as to which lane should be followed for a particular exit. As traffic has increased in recent years the number of smaller roundabouts — mini-roundabouts — has increased significantly. The driver of the LGV must pay particular attention to these roundabouts as the available turning space may be severely constrained and, with a long vehicle, this can lead to serious problems with overhang. As with all other manoeuvres that may be encountered during the LGV test, the examiner will be watching for your general handling of the vehicle and your use of the mirrors and traffic indicators each time a roundabout is approached.

Most roundabouts are one-way systems in which traffic circulates in a clockwise direction. There are also large gyratory roundabouts that can have a two-way traffic flow. This enables double the volume of traffic to use them.

Whatever type of roundabout you are about to enter, you should give way to any traffic approaching from your immediate right (unless the road markings indicate otherwise). To assist the flow of traffic, some roundabouts have traffic lights which determine priority. You should, therefore, look out for road markings, give way signs and traffic signals, and take nothing for granted. The photographic sequences in this chapter illustrate the recommended methods of dealing with roundabouts.

Left:
Roundabouts range in size. The smallest normally encountered are mini-roundabouts, as illustrated here. These are a particular hazard to LGV drivers because of the limited space in which to complete the manoeuvre.

Top left:

The traffic sign informs the driver that there are three mini-roundabouts ahead.

Top right:

This is an aerial view of a large gyratory roundabout which has a two-way traffic system. This arrangement allows double the volume of traffic to use the roundabout. The 'Give Way' rule to traffic on the right applies at each mini-roundabout when travelling in either direction.

Bottom:

When approaching a roundabout use the mirrors so you will be aware of the presence and position of any following traffic. Approach in the left hand lane unless road markings/traffic signs dictate otherwise.

Turning left at a roundabout

Left:

If it is your intention to turn left, then make use of the direction indicators to signal your route to other road users.

Right:

Look to your right so you will see any approaching traffic in good time. Remember that you will have to give way to traffic from the right — including any traffic already on the roundabout — and reduce speed if and when necessary.

Below:

Keep in the left lane, unless directed otherwise.

Far right:

Use the offside mirrors so the presence of any following traffic will be known to you.

Top left:

Use the nearside mirrors. As always, the use of both mirrors should ensure that you are fully aware of the traffic position behind you.

Top right:

Keep to the left lane on the roundabout.

Going ahead at roundabouts

Bottom:

When the hazard is seen check in the mirrors, and look ahead for any road markings.

Top left:
Lose any unwanted speed in good time.

Bottom left:
As you approach the roundabout look to your right in good time.

Far right:
Use the offside mirrors, so that you are aware of any traffic behind you.

Top left:
Follow the left hand lane. As you pass the exit before the one you intend to take, use the left turn indicator.

Turning right or going full circle at roundabouts

Far right:
Look in the mirrors, offside and nearside, so the position and speed of any following traffic will be known to you.

Bottom left:
Use a right turn direction indicator signal, then use the mirrors again and, if safe to do so, move to the right-hand lane.

Top left:

You are now in the correct position on the approach to the roundabout.

Bottom left:

As you approach the roundabout look to your right, so that any approaching traffic will be seen in good time. At some roundabouts your view to the right may be obstructed. You should, therefore, adjust your speed in advance so that you have ample time to pull up should the need arise.

Left:

Look in the mirrors again before the decision to enter the roundabout is made.

16. Roundabouts

Right:
When on the roundabout look in the offside mirrors, so that the position of the trailer can be seen.

Far right:
Then use the nearside mirrors.

Bottom right:
As you approach your exit look to the left. Keep moving if the road ahead of you is clear.

Far left:
Look in your nearside mirror before changing course. An irresponsible car driver can be seen attempting to pass on the nearside.

Top right:
Indicate your intention to turn next left as you pass the exit immediately prior to the one you intend to take.

Bottom right:
Keep moving towards your exit if the way is clear. When you have left the roundabout, look in the mirrors again.

17 Overtaking, meeting and crossing other vehicles

Below:

In this situation the opposing driver has an obstructed road. You have, therefore, no option but to use the mirrors, reduce speed and give way to the approaching traffic.

Below right:

When approaching traffic can be seen as in this situation, you should not use the weight and size of your vehicle to intimidate approaching drivers into giving way, as mentioned opposite.

The examiner will observe your actions when overtaking, meeting other vehicles and crossing the path of other traffic when turning right during the course of the test. Before overtaking, the mirrors must be used to observe any following traffic in good time, and appropriate signals given if necessary.

During a driving test you may have to consider whether to overtake another vehicle. A decision has to be made either to adjust to the road speed of the vehicle and follow it from a safe distance while making reasonable progress, or overtake. A candidate driving an articulated LGV in an urban area may have difficulty at times in deciding whether to overtake, due to the prevailing conditions. If in doubt, hang back until the situation is safe for the manoeuvre.

Meeting other vehicles

While showing consideration for other traffic, you should not exhibit nervousness by giving way unduly to other vehicles when you could be expected to proceed. On the other hand you should not intimidate approaching drivers into giving way by using the weight and size of the vehicle. This also applies when crossing the path of other traffic.

Crossing the path of other traffic

Left:
The driver of the LGV is being inconsiderate by using the weight and size of the vehicle to force approaching drivers into giving way.

18 Signs and road markings

Below:
If a driver ignores the information given on the advanced warning sign, and takes the road leading off to the right at the roundabout, he/she will be committing an offence.

In order to ensure that all road drivers are aware of prevailing road conditions, the highway authorities provide road signs. These signs come in two distinct forms — mandatory and advisory. The former, such as speed limits and no entry, are legally enforceable and, if ignored, lead to a moving vehicle offence and possible prosecution. The advisory signs, such as warnings of low bridges and sharp bends, are designed to draw the driver's attention to hazards in the road ahead. Clearly, the examiner will monitor your response to mandatory signs during the course of the test. As with the ordinary driving test, don't get caught out when the examiner says to take the next available road left by finding yourself endeavouring to turn down a one-way street the wrong way.

The development of road signs started with the arrival of the first motor traffic in the early years of the century. For the first 30 years of this century, motoring organisations had the task of signposting the roads in the United Kingdom. After World War 1, white lines began to appear on the roads of Britain. During the 1920s the use of white lines spread rapidly and, by the 1930s, white lines were used as 'Stop' lines at road junctions controlled either by police or by traffic lights, for marking the course to be taken at bends, junctions and corners, and for indicating the proximity of refuges and other obstacles in the carriageway. In 1934, reflecting studs (cat's eyes) came into use.

New signs introduced in 1933 continued in use until the early 1960s, when the current system of road signs was adopted. By 1965 all the 'regulatory' signs giving commands or prohibitions were introduced to the United Kingdom. These signs, which adopted standard European designs, are applied universally on Britain's roads. The variety of signs, signals and road markings we have today convey their information quickly and accurately, but to be of any use the driver must understand the message they give, otherwise lives could be in danger. Traffic signs and road markings, combined with signals given by other road users, are the language of the road. It is disturbing but true that the average road user does not see or understand the majority of road signs provided for his/her guidance.

There are some signs that direct drivers of LGVs to a particular route, and others prohibit the use of some roads. It should also be noted that certain advisory signs, such as those warning of humpbacked bridges where there is a danger of grounding, are of more immediate interest to drivers of LGVs than to the majority of road users. A selection of signs is shown here.

Left:
The sign gives a clear mandatory message.

Below left:
If the information on the sign is not complied with the consequence could be expensive.

Top left:
To all intents and purposes, you may think the road leading off to the right can be used by LGVs.

Bottom:
It is not until you leave the roundabout that you learn otherwise.

Top right:
No PCVs (Passenger Carrying Vehicles) or LGVs.

Far left:
**No vehicles over 40ft
allowed, except for access.**

Above:
**To protect this bridge from
overloading, a weight limit of
17 tonnes applies.**

Left:
**The information given is
clear and precise.**

Right:
Should a driver take the next road on the right, the sign informs him there is a weight limit one mile from the junction.

Far right:
The next road on the right has a width limit and is a no through route.

Far left:
LGVs that have an axle weight of over 3 tonnes must comply with the sign.

Left:
The message given on the sign is clear. MGW stands for Maximum Gross Weight.

Right:

These signs inform drivers of LGVs to travel on a lorry route. By doing so they will avoid roads that have weight limits.

Far right:

If there is a lane designated for traffic turning right, and the lane is longer than the vehicle being driven, try to position your vehicle in the lane provided. This will enable the driver to avoid obstructing the nearside lane.

19 Conclusion of the test

At the end of the test drive you will be back at the test centre. At this point the examiner will direct you to a place where you can pull up. When the vehicle has been brought to rest, apply the hand-brake and return the gear lever to the neutral position. The examiner will ask you to stop the engine. You will then be asked some questions on the *Highway Code* and other motoring matters. In 1994 the oral examination will cease and a written theoretical examination will be instituted in its place. It is important that the candidate is well versed in the subject through reading the *Highway Code* and other books on motoring skills.

The following are a representative selection of the questions which could be put to you. These are not intended to provide a full guide to the questions asked (either verbally or in the written test) but are designed to provide you with an idea about the content of the question and the type of response required.

● 1. Q. **What factors should be taken into consideration in selecting a suitable place to leave an uncoupled semi-trailer?**

A. Select a position where the trailer will not cause danger or inconvenience to any other road user.

● 2. Q. **What are the important factors in selecting a suitable surface for uncoupling?**

A. Select a firm hard surface on level ground. This reduces the risk of movement and prevents any possible strain on brakes and/or suspension.

● 3. Q. **Detail the order in which you would carry out the operations necessary to uncouple a trailer from a tractor unit.**

A. a. Secure the trailer brakes in the 'on' position.
b. Lower front trailer legs (or wheels) and lock in position.
c. Disconnect airlines and electrical connections.

d. Release coupling.
e. Drive tractor unit slowly away.

● 4. Q. **On recoupling what safety check should be made to ensure that unit and trailer are securely coupled?**

A. Attempt to drive forward with trailer brake on.

● 5. Q. **If the air line connections to the trailer have self-sealed valves, what special checks must be made?**

A. After reconnecting the brake lines, check that the trailer is receiving air from the tractor unit.

● 6. Q. **How can you check that the trailer is receiving air from the tractor unit?**

A. Air should be heard flowing through the emergency line (red) when it is connected. Apply the footbrake and, when released, air will be heard discharging from the trailer.

● 7. Q. **How should the landing gear be secured in the 'up' position?**

A. With the handle in the 'stowed' position.

● 8. Q. **What is the correct order in which recoupling should be carried out?**

A. a. Check that the trailer parking brake is applied.
b. Check the height of the turntable in relation to the king pin.
c. Reverse tractor unit slowly into coupled position.
d. Ensure unit is securely coupled by attempting to move forward with trailer parking brake applied.
e. Connect braking and electrical connections.
f. Secure front trailer legs (or wheels) in the 'up' position.
g. Release trailer parking brake.
h. Make sure all electrics (lights) on the trailer work.

● **9. Q. On returning to your vehicle after lunch (which you have had in a transport café), what should you do before getting into the vehicle?**

A. Look round the vehicle and check that the load is secure in order to make sure that nothing has been tampered with.

● **10. Q. What should you do to ensure the load is safe?**

A. You should check that the distribution of the load is even, that the height of the vehicle and load are suitable, that there is no overlapping and that the load is well secured in the event of emergency braking.

● **11. Q. If the vehicle is fitted with air brakes, why is it dangerous to coast downhill?**

A. Air pressure may not build up as the engine is only ticking over. This is a particular problem if the vehicle is fitted with a badly worn compressor.

● **12. Q. What are the most usual warning devices on air or vacuum braked vehicles?**

A. The most usual devices are a warning light, a flag signal, a pressure gauge or a buzzer.

● **13. Q. What is the two-speed axle or splitter gear?**

A. A further gear fitted to the back axle or gearbox which, when controlled by the driver, doubles the number of gears available.

● **14. Q. With air brakes, what is generally a safe minimum pressure?**

A. 45-60lb/sq in (3-4.5bar).

After the examiner has finished asking you questions like these, he/she will then inform you whether you have passed or failed. The appropriate paperwork will also be completed and handed over at this point. If you have passed, congratulations; if you have failed, the examiner's report will highlight those areas which were considered unsatisfactory.

20 Don't be a bridge basher

Not only does bridge bashing imperil lives, it is always costly. Bridge repair work costs anything from a few hundred pounds to hundreds of thousands of pounds for complete replacement. Any structural repair is expensive — but just think of the cost of replacing a whole bridge. Insurance companies don't enjoy having to pay out millions of pounds a year to repair damaged bridges. It will be the firm for which you work that will be paying the price, in much higher insurance premiums, in expensive and time-intensive repairs to vehicle bodywork and even in lost driving jobs. Bridge bashing also creates traffic chaos, and can disrupt railway services — and makes the driver look stupid. A lorry wedged under a bridge can take most of a day to remove — blocking the road and causing severe disruption on the roads and railways. You may well have been caught up in this kind of traffic hold-up before. The majority

of low bridges are well signposted in advance and will have the height prominently displayed on the actual structure but, if you find a bridge height which is not clearly marked, please call British Rail Works Group on 0345 581657; they will appreciate your call.

Problems of this nature can be avoided by the careful preparation of the route plan in advance to avoid known low bridges, by a proper appreciation of the height of the vehicle and (more importantly) its load and by following the guidance from road signs. An LGV driver should be particularly watchful when the margin is tight; inevitably there can be inaccuracies in the measurement of the low bridge, especially when road resurfacing work has increased the road level slightly. If in doubt, it always pays to avoid the low bridge concerned.

Below left:
There is a low bridge beyond the roundabout. Should your vehicle be too high, amber lights will start flashing and a message will be shown informing you that your vehicle is too tall to go under the bridge.

Below:
The exit from this bridge is very narrow — indicated by the road markings in the centre of the bridge — and the driver must be aware of the potential dangers at this point.

21 Spot-checks and the law

After passing the LGV driving test you may wish to drive an LGV as a full-time job. Possession of an LGV licence qualifies you to drive all vehicles in the appropriate category (and nowadays Category C includes multiwheelers) and, thus, will give you the freedom of the road. However, it remains your responsibility to ensure that the vehicle you are driving and the load being transported are, and will remain, safe. There are a number of statutory authorities which have powers to stop your vehicle and undertake spot checks. As recession and cost-cutting affects companies, particularly in the road haulage business, there is a temptation to reduce maintenance and overload vehicles. Always remember that if you are caught with an illegal vehicle, you stand to lose both your hard-earned licence as well as any financial penalty resulting from the infringement.

The general purpose of spot checks on vehicles is to improve road safety. It is recognised by the authorities that there are a number of drivers who use the roads in the United Kingdom, knowing that a defective vehicle is being driven. There are some drivers who are not aware that a potentially dangerous vehicle is being driven, until they are stopped and the vehicle is checked. Unfortunately, ignorance is no legal defence — it is your responsibility as driver to ensure the condition of both vehicle and load. Some drivers may be largely innocent, whilst others try to evade the law. Unfortunately all will be treated the same if discovered committing an illegality.

Right:
A police officer signals a driver to slow down, and directs him into the entrance of the checking area.

Left:
The police officer informs the driver that the vehicle and documentation are going to be checked.

Bottom left:
This vehicle has just entered the checking area. The driver has been asked to stop the vehicle on the weighbridge, where the weight of the vehicle/load will be checked. Once in the checking area, staff from the Department of Transport take over.

Bottom right:
When the weight of the vehicle has been checked, the driver will be asked to produce the appropriate documentation appertaining to the vehicle and the load being carried.

Top left:
**The Road Fund tax disc is
then checked.**

Bottom:
**The fuel is then checked by
an officer from HM Custom &
Excise. The purpose of this
check is to make sure that
illegal diesel fuel is not being
used. Untaxed fuel, used for
agricultural, marine and
other purposes, is dyed red,
and use of red diesel in vehicles on the road is an
offence.**

Top right:
**A vehicle examiner has found
a mechanical fault on the
front nearside wheel.**